HOUSE OF PUZZLES

WORD
PUZZLES

THIS IS A CARLTON BOOK

Published by Carlton Books Ltd
20 Mortimer Street
London W1T 3JW

Copyright © 2011 Carlton Books Ltd

A CIP catalogue for this book is available from the British Library.

ISBN 978-1-84732-855-7

Printed and bound by CPI Group (UK) Ltd, Croydon, CR0 4YY

Some of the puzzles in this book were previously published in *House of Puzzles Killer Crosswords*

HOUSE OF PUZZLES

WORD PUZZLES

Over 200 superb puzzles to challenge
your logic and word power

CARLTON

Word Puzzles

Word puzzles have a long and glorious tradition in all literate societies. Some of the earliest ones we have found so far date back to the ancient Greeks, who were very fond of their riddles.

You'll find a wide selection of different puzzle types inside this book – everything from antonym challenges and analogies through to crafty ciphers to decode. Several of the puzzle types owe their birth to Lewis Carroll, still one of the greatest puzzlers that the United Kingdom has produced. Symbolic logic tangles, to pick one example.

If there's a puzzle type that you find tricky, I'd encourage you not to just skip it. Those encounters are your best opportunities to develop your puzzling skills. Stick with it, and you may find that what was baffling suddenly becomes clear.

Have fun, and happy puzzling.
Tim Dedopulos

PUZZLE 1

ANALOGY

Follow the logic of the first pair to find the closest corresponding option to complete the second pair.

GIBBON is to PRIMATES as DOG is to:

a. Canine
b. Singulata
c. Carnivora
d. Lupus

PUZZLE 2

ANTONYM

Which of the six options is closest to an opposite meaning of the word below?

DESOLATION

boon
security
dolor
gratification
joy
fruition

CIPHER

The block of text below represents a quote that has been encrypted using a simple cipher. Can you decrypt it? You shouldn't need to use a computer to solve this puzzle, although there are some web sites that would help.

ALLTR	ULYWI	SETHO	UGHTS	HAVEB	EENTH
OUGHT	ALREA	DYTHO	USAND	SOFTI	MESBU
TTOMA	KETHE	MTRUL	YOURS	WEMUS	TTHIN
KTHEM	OVERA	GAINH	ONEST	LYTIL	LTHEY
TAKER	OOTIN	OURPE	RSONA	LEXPE	RIENC
EJOHA	NNWOL	FGANG	VONGO	ETHEX	

CUT-UP

The lines below form a quotation attributed to a famous individual. Full-stops and commas have been removed, and the lines jumbled up. Can you piece the original quotation back together?

ARTICLE OF MERE CONSUMPTION

AS A HOUSE FOR HUNDREDS OF

BUT FAIRLY OF CAPITAL AND

YEARS IT IS NOT THEN AN

IS THEIR ONLY CAPITAL

BOOKS CONSTITUTE CAPITAL A

MEN SETTING OUT IN LIFE IT

LIBRARY BOOK LASTS AS LONG

OFTEN IN THE CASE OF PROFESSIONAL

Thomas Jefferson

DITLOID

A well-known phrase or title has been reduced to numbers and abbreviations in the clue below. Can you decipher the answer?

7 = W of the AW

DOUBLET

Change one letter at a time to form a new valid English word until you have transformed the first word into the second word.

There are 4 interim stages.

Head

Tail

PUZZLE 7

FOUR FROM FOUR

Within the four words below, four smaller words are hiding. What is the theme that unites them?

Infantilism

Wildebeest

Politicking

Smothering

PUZZLE 8

GAP-WORD

Which word will add to the two words below, to the end of the former and the beginning of the latter, to make two new words?

Altar — ? — Meal

GRIDRUNNER

Starting from one spot in the grid below, move from letter to letter horizontally, vertically or diagonally to touch every letter once and spell out the name of a well-known person.

HOLE

Fit a letter into the gap to complete four five-letter words.

CA___YX

BA___MS

TA___US

HE___OT

PUZZLE 11

INTERMINGLING

Three loosely related words or phrases have been mixed together below. They are still in the right order, but each is scrambled with the other two. What are they?

```
TINSOTEHUERNAATHRTICERTONN
ICALDAHECMITISEPRLHEINCLEREE
```

PUZZLE 12

JUMBLE

The letters below form a well-known quotation. Each word has been anagrammed, and then the punctuation and spaces have been removed. The words are still in their correct places, however. Can you work out what the original quotation was? To help, we've given you the quotation's author.

```
NOEMRTTAWHOLNOGHELSIEVNOA
NMVEREOBCESMESASIEWASH-
ET        GEEVAAROWANMOFRTOFYHIEGT
```

H. L. Mencken

KIN

In this puzzle, you have a group of five related words. One word in the other group belongs with them. Which one is it?

APPROBATE	handle
CHAMPION	seal
EULOGIZE	choose
SANCTION	uphold
SPONSOR	acquiesce

LETTERS

Rearrange the letters to form a single eight-letter word.

S
C
O
R
N
G
Y
E

PUZZLE **15**

LOGIC

Consider the statements below, and assuming that they are all perfectly true, answer the question that follows.

- I despise anything that cannot be used as a bridge.
- Everything that is worth writing a poem to would be a welcome gift to me.
- A rainbow will not bear the weight of a wheelbarrow.
- Whatever can be used as a bridge will bear the weight of a wheelbarrow.
- I would not take a thing that I despise as a gift.

How are worthy poem topics and rainbows logically related?

PUZZLE **16**

ODD ONE OUT

Which of the following words does not fit with the other four – and why? The answer lies in the words' meanings.

Accuse

Allege

Appeal

Attribute

Arraign

PREFIXES

Which word can be added to the front of the following words to make five new whole words?

Static

Pics

Film

Available

Tins

SCRAMBLE

Remove one letter from each group in turn, going round three times, to spell out three different ten-letter words without re-using any letters.

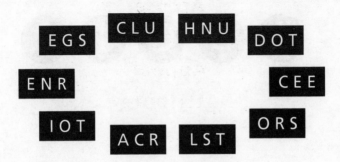

PUZZLE **19**

SELECTOR

Starting anywhere, pick one letter from each group in turn, clockwise, to find a ten-letter word loosely associated with the building industry.

PUZZLE **20**

SEQUENCES

Work out the rationale behind the following sequence of letters and find the next one in the list.

SYZYGY

Transform the first word into the second by moving from word to word. Each new word, or syzygy, must share a continuous group of at least three letters – the 'link' – with the word before it.

Abbreviations, names, foreign words, compound words and slang are all forbidden. Consecutive links may overlap by a maximum of one letter, and similarly you may only use one letter of common suffixes and prefixes – such as '-ing', '-ers' or 'un-' – in a link. No syzygies may be longer than 11 letters.

There are 2 in-between syzygies.

Walrus

Carpenter

PUZZLE **22**

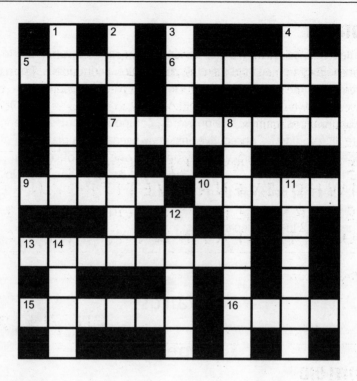

Across

- **5.** Daybreak (4)
- **6.** Empty (6)
- **7.** Writhing (8)
- **9.** Audio-only broadcast (5)
- **10.** Bonelike structure in the jaw (5)
- **13.** Bouncing Aussie mammal (8)
- **15.** Reflexive third-person pronoun (6)
- **16.** Donated (4)

Down

- **1.** Country north of mainland America (6)
- **2.** Turning yarn into garments (8)
- **3.** Seat (5)
- **4.** Dispirited (4)
- **8.** Exhaustive (8)
- **11.** Days of Christmas (6)
- **12.** Trade (5)
- **14.** Behaves (4)

JUMBLE

The letters below form a well-known quotation. Each word has been anagrammed, and then the punctuation and spaces have been removed. The words are still in their correct places, however. Can you work out what the original quotation was? To help, we've given you the quotation's author.

```
E V I T O G A N O G L T L S I F O O O B S K I S
I W H D I E V E N R N W E T I T R D A N V E I
E K T P M E H T A L L U T O F O T P I N R R
O F H T E S T A P N W E Y T T R E Y A S
```

Dean Koontz

DITLOID

A well-known phrase or title has been reduced to numbers and abbreviations in the clue below. Can you decipher the answer?

$$7 = S$$

PUZZLE 25

PREFIXES

Which word can be added to the front of the following words to make five new whole words?

Cap

Tab

Worm

Reach

Set

PUZZLE 26

SEQUENCES

Work out the rationale behind the following sequence of letters and find the next one in the list.

H

H E

L I B

E B

?

ANALOGY

Follow the logic of the first pair to find the closest corresponding option to complete the second pair.

GOLD is to MERCURY as SILVER is to:

a. Copper
b. Cadmium
c. Zinc
d. Palladium

PUZZLE **28**

ANTONYM

Which of the six options is closest to an opposite meaning of the word below?

ENTHETIC

internal
ventilated
established
pioneering
greenish
approving

CIPHER

The block of text below represents a quotation that has been encrypted using a simple cipher. Can you decrypt it? You shouldn't need to use a computer to solve this puzzle, although there are some web sites that would help.

BOZPOF XIP TUPQT MFBSOJOH JT PME

XIFUIFS BU UXFOUZ PS FJHIUZ BOZPOF

XIP LFFQT MFBSOJOH TUBZT ZPVOH UIF

HSFBUFTU UIJOH JO MJGF JT UP LFFQ

ZPVS NJOE ZPVOH IFOSZ GPSE

CUT-UP

The lines below form a quotation attributed to a famous individual.
Full-stops and commas have been removed, and the lines jumbled
up. Can you piece the original quotation back together?

BEING OBLIGED BY BETTER

OPINIONS EVEN ON IMPORTANT

CONSIDERATION TO CHANGE

EXPERIENCED MANY INSTANCES OF

FOR HAVING LIVED LONG I HAVE

INFORMATION OR FULLER

RIGHT BUT FOUND TO BE OTHERWISE

SUBJECTS WHICH I ONCE THOUGHT

Benjamin Franklin

PUZZLE **31**

DITLOID

A well-known phrase or title has been reduced to numbers and abbreviations in the clue below. Can you decipher the answer?

3 = M in a B

PUZZLE **32**

DOUBLET

Change one letter at a time to form a new valid English word until you have transformed the first word into the second word.

There are 4 interim stages.

Ape

Man

FOUR FROM FOUR

Within the four words below, four smaller words are hiding. What is the theme that unites them?

Solidification

Comedogenic

Epigrammatic

Erratically

GAP-WORD

Which word will add to the two words below, to the end of the former and the beginning of the latter, to make two new words?

Baby — ? — Reps

PUZZLE **35**

GRIDRUNNER

Starting from one spot in the grid below, move from letter to letter horizontally, vertically or diagonally to touch every letter once and spell out the name of a well-known person.

N	E	O	S	W
C	I	S	F	A
R	A	I	D	L
P	A	N	E	S

PUZZLE **36**

HOLE

Fit a letter into the gap to complete four five-letter words.

CA__ED

EA__ER

SA__OS

GI__UE

INTERMINGLING

Three loosely related words or phrases have been mixed together below. They are still in the right order, but each is scrambled with the other two. What are they?

```
A E O T U U P L B U I A R I L A N R
B G H H T P E I A L L R A N P S O
```

JUMBLE

The letters below form a well-known quotation. Each word has been anagrammed, and then the punctuation and spaces have been removed. The words are still in their correct places, however. Can you work out what the original quotation was? To help, we've given you the quotation's author.

```
S A O G L N A S O Y E R U N I O G N O T E B
I H I N K T N G A A Y W N Y N T K H I I G B
```

Donald Trump

PUZZLE **39**

KIN

In this puzzle, you have a group of five related words. One word in the other group belongs with them. Which one is it?

FIEF · suzerainty

DEMESNE · Elysium

ARENA · stretch

BAILIWICK · polity

DOMINION · scope

PUZZLE **40**

LETTERS

Rearrange the letters to form a single eight-letter word.

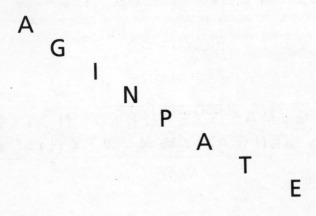

A
G
I
N
P
A
T
E

LOGIC

Consider the statements below, and assuming that they are all perfectly true, answer the question that follows.

- These Sorite logic examples are not arranged in regular order, like the examples I am used to.
- When I can solve a logic example without grumbling, you may be sure it is one that I can understand.
- No easy example ever makes my head ache.
- I can't understand examples that are not arranged in regular order, like those I am used to.
- I never grumble at an example, unless it gives me a headache.

How are the Sorites and difficulty logically related?

ODD ONE OUT

Which of the following words does not fit with the other four – and why? The answer lies in the words' meanings.

Fletcherize

Murmalize

Absquatulate

Subtilize

Yaff

PREFIXES

Which word can be added to the front of the following words to make five new whole words?

Bolt

Like

Worm

Toss

Git

PUZZLE **44**

SCRAMBLE

Remove one letter from each group in turn, going round three times, to spell out three different ten-letter words without re-using any letters.

SELECTOR

Starting anywhere, pick one letter from each group in turn, clockwise, to find a ten-letter word loosely associated with office work.

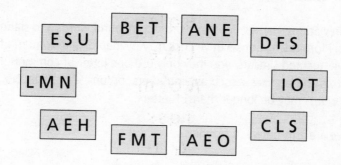

SEQUENCES

Work out the rationale behind the following sequence of letters and find the next one in the list.

T F S E

T T F

?

PUZZLE **47**

SYZYGY

Transform the first word into the second by moving from word to word. Each new word must share a continuous group of at least three letters – the 'link' – with the word before it.

Abbreviations, names, foreign words, compound words and slang are all forbidden. Consecutive links may overlap by a maximum of one letter, and similarly you may only use one letter of common suffixes and prefixes – such as '-ing', '-ers' or 'un-' – in a link. No link words may be longer than 11 letters.

There are 2 in-between syzygies.

Indulge

Idiosyncrasy

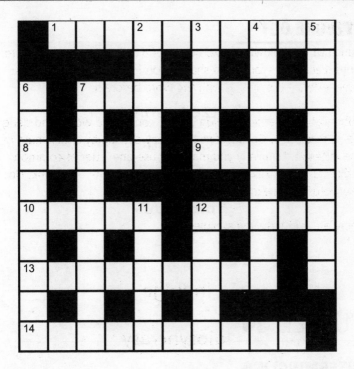

Across

1. Part of a hundred (10)
7. Earnestly (9)
8. Judging committee (5)
9. Something that happens (5)
10. Not the same (5)
12. High quality porcelain (5)
13. Going to (9)
14. Line of descent (10)

Down

2. Colourful reef creature (5)
3. Nobody (2-3)
4. Responding (9)
5. Builders of the pyramids (9)
6. International negotiators (9)
7. Man-made (9)
11. Reach (5)
12. Metal currency tokens (5)

PUZZLE **49**

ODD ONE OUT

Which of the following words do not fit with the other four – and why?

Katzenjammer

Quixotic

Syzygy

Beziques

Tarts

PUZZLE **50**

INTERMINGLING

Three loosely related words or phrases have been mixed together below. They are still in the right order, but each is scrambled with the other two. What are they?

| M M P O R E N A U K N S I E U Y N R W |
| I G S N R G H E E T A N A C P R E S H |

SCRAMBLE

Remove one letter from each group in turn, going round three times, to spell out three different ten-letter words without re-using any letters.

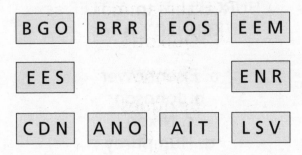

LOGIC

Consider the statements below, and assuming that they are all perfectly true, answer the question that follows.

- All the human race, except footmen, have a certain amount of common sense.
- No one who lives on barley-sugar can be anything but a mere baby.
- None but a hop-scotch player knows what real happiness is.
- No mere baby has a grain of common sense.
- No driver ever plays hop-scotch.
- No footman is ignorant of what true happiness is.

How are drivers and barley-sugar logically related?

PUZZLE **53**

ANALOGY

Follow the logic of the first pair to find the closest corresponding option to complete the second pair.

CHURCHILL is to ATTLEE as KENNEDY is to:

a. Eisenhower
b. Johnson
c. Nixon
d. Humphrey

PUZZLE **54**

ANTONYM

Which of the six options is closest to an opposite meaning of the word below?

PREDICATE

stress
ravage
suppress
invalidate
destroy
drain

CIPHER

The block of text below represents a quotation that has been encrypted using a simple cipher. Can you decrypt it? You shouldn't need to use a computer to solve this puzzle, although there are some web sites that would help.

RJ GNIK REHTUL NITRAM LLEW BOJ SIH DID

OHW REPEEWS TEERTS TAERG A DEVIL EREH

YAS DNA ESUAP LLIW HTRAE DNA NEVAEH FO

STSOH EHT LLA TAHT LLEW OS STEERTS PEEWS

DLUOHS EH YRTEOP ETORW ERAEPSEKAHS RO

CISUM DESOPMOC NEVOHTEEB RO DETNIAP OLEGNA

LEHCIM SA NEVE STEERTS PEEWS DLUOHS EH

REPEEWS TEERTS A EB OT DELLAC SI NAM A FI

PUZZLE 56

Across

6. Talked over (9)
7. Metal-bearing mineral (3)
8. Residue from burning (3)
9. Fruit of the ficus (3)
11. Not specialized (7)
13. Long, flat snow-runner (3)
14. A hard-shelled seed (3)
16. Pixie (3)
17. Outline of a shore (9)

Down

1. Nominates (8)
2. Lazy (4)
3. The largest continent (4)
4. Professional book-writer (6)
5. Handy (6)
10. Small orange-red aquarium fish (8)
11. 6-stringed instrument (6)
12. Music for nine voices (6)
15. A duplicate copy (4)
16. Looked at (4)

CUT-UP

The lines below form a quotation attributed to a famous individual. Full-stops and commas have been removed, and the lines jumbled up. Can you piece the original quotation back together?

AVOIDING DANGER IS NO SAFER

SECURITY IS MOSTLY A

THE CHILDREN OF MEN AS A

EXIST IN NATURE NOR DO

IN THE LONG RUN THAN OUTRIGHT

DARING ADVENTURE OR NOTHING

EXPOSURE LIFE IS EITHER A

SUPERSTITION IT DOES NOT

WHOLE EXPERIENCE IT

Hellen Keller

PUZZLE **58**

DITLOID

A well-known phrase or title has been reduced to numbers and abbreviations in the clue below. Can you decipher the answer?

$$12 = L \text{ of } H$$

PUZZLE **59**

DOUBLET

Change one letter at a time to form a new valid English word until you have transformed the first word into the second word.

There are 5 interim stages.

Sleep

Dream

FOUR FROM FOUR

Within the four words below, four smaller words are hiding. What is the theme that unites them?

Yarmulkes

Linearity

Solipsistic

Allegedly

GAP-WORD

Which word will add to the two words below, to the end of the former and the beginning of the latter, to make two new words?

Red — ? — Spring

PUZZLE **62**

GRIDRUNNER

Starting from one spot in the grid below, move from letter to letter horizontally, vertically or diagonally to touch every letter once and spell out the name of a well-known person.

PUZZLE **63**

HOLE

Fit a letter into the gap to complete four five-letter words.

MO__ED

KA__OK

RE__OT

AS__IC

INTERMINGLING

Three loosely related words or phrases have been mixed together below. They are still in the right order, but each is scrambled with the other two. What are they?

| B | H | O | M | I | U | N | A | R | D | C | T | I | N | I | N | G | G | R | O |
| L | O | A | H | O | P | A | R | D | T | U | G | M | S | E | E | N | E | T |

JUMBLE

The letters below form a well-known quotation. Each word has been anagrammed, and then the punctuation and spaces have been removed. The words are still in their correct places, however. Can you work out what the original quotation was? To help, we've given you the quotation's author.

A	N	Y	M	A	P	I	R	T	O	N	N	T	U	I	S	E	C	O
L	G	N	E	F	R	T	A	V	M	M	E	N	E	O	T	M	T
E	I	E	P	A	S	C	H	V	E	A	S	A	D	C	E	E

John Steinbeck

PUZZLE **66**

KIN

In this puzzle, you have a group of five related words. One word in the other group belongs with them. Which one is it?

CLOTHAR	Iskander
ALFRED	Sigurd
ALEXANDER	Mehmed
PETER	Mircea
TAMBURLAINE	Sargon

PUZZLE **67**

LETTERS

Rearrange the letters to form a single eight-letter word.

B
A
G
I
S
T
B
N

LOGIC

Consider the statements below, and assuming that they are all perfectly true, answer the question that follows.

- Every idea of mine, that cannot be expressed as a Syllogism, is really ridiculous.
- None of my ideas about Bath-buns are worth writing down.
- No idea of mine, that fails to come true, can be expressed as a Syllogism.
- I never have any really ridiculous idea, that I do not at once refer to my solicitor.
- My dreams are all about Bath-buns.
- I never refer any idea of mine to my solicitor, unless it is worth writing down.

How are my dreams and coming true related?

ODD ONE OUT

Which of the following words does not fit with the other four – and why? The answer lies in the words' meanings.

Lozenge

Solidus

Bang

Pilcrow

Carrel

PUZZLE **70**

PREFIXES

Which word can be added to the front of the following words to make five new whole words?

Berry

Nuts

Ants

On

Stone

PUZZLE **71**

SCRAMBLE

Remove one letter from each group in turn, going round three times, to spell out three different ten-letter words without re-using any letters.

SELECTOR

Starting anywhere, pick one letter from each group in turn, clockwise, to find a ten-letter word loosely associated with words.

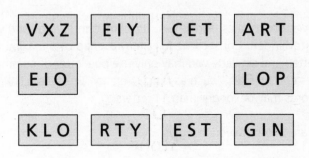

SEQUENCES

Work out the rationale behind the following sequence of letters and find the next one in the list.

D N

O S A

J ?

PUZZLE **74**

SYZYGY

Transform the first word into the second by moving from word to word. Each new word must share a continuous group of at least three letters – the 'link' – with the word before it.

Abbreviations, names, foreign words, compound words and slang are all forbidden. Consecutive links may overlap by a maximum of one letter, and similarly you may only use one letter of common suffixes and prefixes – such as '-ing', '-ers' or 'un-' – in a link. No link words may be longer than 11 letters.

There are 2 in-between syzygies.

Cook

Dinner

Across

4. Shopping (9)
6. Ease up (6)
7. Serving girl (4)
8. Foot switch (5)
10. Rumours (5)
12. Weaponry (4)
13. Reckon (6)
15. Red (9)

Down

1. Diaries (4)
2. Finances (5)
3. Unhappiness (6)
4. Shaped (9)
5. Merest (9)
9. Conclude (6)
11. Howl (5)
14. Brace (4)

PUZZLE **76**

JUMBLE

The letters below form a well-known quotation. Each word has been anagrammed, and then the punctuation and spaces have been removed. The words are still in their correct places, however. Can you work out what the original quotation was? To help, we've given you the quotation's author.

EHTRENHGTISOCNTANEBOGNLNDHE
IDTEHNSUHTEOMNNONDAHETRUHTT

Buddha

PUZZLE **77**

DITLOID

A well-known phrase or title has been reduced to numbers and abbreviations in the clue below. Can you decipher the answer?

4 = H of the A

PREFIXES

Which word can be added to the front of the following words to make five new whole words?

Ding

Rid

Dens

Wort

Cap

SEQUENCES

Work out the rationale behind the following sequence of letters and find the next one in the list.

A

B C

C D E

E ?

PUZZLE **80**

ANALOGY

Follow the logic of the first pair to find the closest corresponding option to complete the second pair.

BREAKAGE is to LOSS as IRRIGATION is to:

a. Trade
b. Swamp
c. Crop
d. Tundra

PUZZLE **81**

ANTONYM

Which of the six options is closest to an opposite meaning of the word below?

NOOSE

redeem

exculpate

grab

assume

liberate

mimic

CIPHER

The block of text below represents a quotation that has been
encrypted using a simple cipher. Can you decrypt it? You shouldn't
need to use a computer to solve this puzzle, although there are
some web sites that would help.

```
UVFGBEL FUBJF HF GUNG GUR CRBCYR
JUB RAQ HC PUNATVAT GUR JBEYQ GUR
TERNG CBYVGVPNY FBPVNY FPVRAGVS VP
GRPUABYBTVPNY NEGVFGVP RIRA FCBEGF
ERIBYHGVBANEVRF NER NYJNL F AHGF
HAGVY GURL NER EVTUG NAQ GURA
GURL NER TRAVHFRF WBUA RYVBG
```

PUZZLE **83**

CUT-UP

The lines below form a quotation attributed to a famous individual.
Full-stops and commas have been removed, and the lines jumbled up.
Can you piece the original quotation back together?

A LONG PLASTIC HALLWAY WHERE

FOR NO GOOD REASON

KIND OF CRUEL AND SHALLOW

NORMALLY PERCEIVED AS SOME

AND GOOD MEN DIE LIKE DOGS

OF THE JOURNALISM INDUSTRY

THAN MOST THINGS IT IS

THIEVES AND PIMPS RUN FREE

THE TV BUSINESS IS UGLIER

MONEY TRENCH THROUGH THE HEART

Hunter S. Thompson

DITLOID

A well-known phrase or title has been reduced to numbers and abbreviations in the clue below. Can you decipher the answer?

2 = G of V

DOUBLET

Change one letter at a time to form a new valid English word until you have transformed the first word into the second word.

There are 5 interim stages.

Flour

Bread

PUZZLE 86

FOUR FROM FOUR

Within the four words below, four smaller words are hiding. What is the theme that unites them?

Acrobacterium

Discontent

Burgundies

Excellently

PUZZLE 87

GAP-WORD

Which word will add to the two words below, to the end of the former and the beginning of the latter, to make two new words?

Hack — ? — Like

GRIDRUNNER

Starting from one spot in the grid below, move from letter
to letter horizontally, vertically or diagonally to touch every
letter once and spell out the name of a well-known person.

T	R	R	J	G	N
I	A	T	U	E	I
M	N	L	H	K	R

PUZZLE **89**

HOLE

Fit a letter into the gap to complete four five-letter words.

SA__OT

DE__AR

EM__OW

RE__US

INTERMINGLING

Three loosely related words or phrases have been mixed together below. They are still in the right order, but each is scrambled with the other two. What are they?

THETVERIELROCOCDOIENT
RORASAUARPTTOOPURSS

PUZZLE **91**

JUMBLE

The letters below form a well-known quotation. Each word has been anagrammed, and then the punctuation and spaces have been removed. The words are still in their correct places, however. Can you work out what the original quotation was? To help, we've given you the quotation's author.

ASSIAALETOSSIFIELONT
HWOGOLNTIISTUBWHOO
OGDITSIISHWTATARMEST

Lucius Annaeus Seneca

KIN

In this puzzle, you have a group of five related words. One word in the other group belongs with them. Which one is it?

CROHN	Fort
HUNTINGDON	Jakob
TOURETTE	Seebeck
ADDISON	Cray
DOWN	Wade

LETTERS

Rearrange the letters to form a single eight-letter word.

I
T
S
S
A
A
D
D

PUZZLE **94**

LOGIC

Consider the statements below, and assuming that they are all perfectly true, answer the question that follows.

- None of the pictures here, except the battle-pieces, are valuable.
- None of the unframed ones are varnished.
- All the battle-pieces are painted in oils.
- All those that have been sold are valuable.
- All the English pictures are varnished.
- All those pictures in frames have been sold.

How are the English pictures here and oil paintings related?

PUZZLE **95**

ODD ONE OUT

Which of the following terms does not fit with the other four – and why? The answer lies in the terms' meanings.

The same boat

Catch 22

The same page

Hot potato

The brunt

PREFIXES

Which word can be added to the front of the following words to make five new whole words?

Marine

Sonic

High

Modern

Conservative

SCRAMBLE

Remove one letter from each group in turn, going round three times, to spell out three different ten-letter words without re-using any letters.

A H W	A D I	N R U	D E L

D D S			C H T

E E E	F I R	F I R	A E U

PUZZLE **98**

SELECTOR

Starting anywhere, pick one letter from each group in turn, clockwise, to find a ten-letter word loosely associated with the Far East.

PUZZLE **99**

SEQUENCES

Work out the rationale behind the following sequence of letters and find the next one in the list.

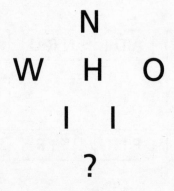

SYZYGY

Transform the first word into the second by moving from word to word. Each new word must share a continuous group of at least three letters – the 'link' – with the word before it.

Abbreviations, names, foreign words, compound words and slang are all forbidden. Consecutive links may overlap by a maximum of one letter, and similarly you may only use one letter of common suffixes and prefixes – such as '-ing', '-ers' or 'un-' – in a link. No link words may be longer than 11 letters.

There are 2 in-between syzygies.

Knife

Fork

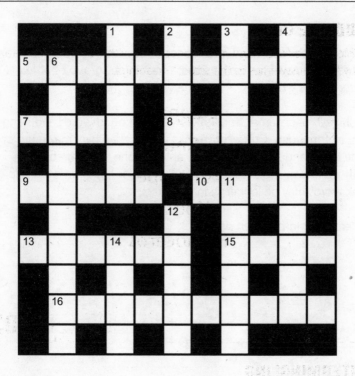

Across

5. Drawing the windspeed (10)
7. Yeast floats in sherry (4)
8. Daydream on the run (6)
9. Taman ancients (5)
10. Glacier-facing (5)
13. Coiled round (6)
15. Dirty oaf (4)
16. Announces the solo artist (10)

Down

1. Simply suffocated (6)
2. The most common African lizard (5)
3. Real good Hindi God-singer (4)
4. Flash bang fever (10)
6. Making zero (10)
11. Small, broad and wellhammered (6)
12. Pair of minced devils (5)
14. Directs schemes (4)

ODD ONE OUT

Which of the following words does not fit with the other four – and why? The answer lies in the words' meanings.

Elephant

Gaur

Antelope

Kodiak

Rhinoceros

INTERMINGLING

Three loosely related words or phrases have been mixed together below. They are still in the right order, but each is scrambled with the other two. What are they?

W E P E L S L A L I P T N F A G T D O R
O N R M I S L H B O L O E E O S S T S

PUZZLE **104**

SCRAMBLE

Remove one letter from each group in turn, going round three times, to spell out three different ten-letter words without re-using any letters.

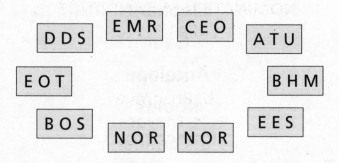

PUZZLE **105**

LOGIC

Consider the statements below, and assuming that they are all perfectly true, answer the question that follows.

- I trust every animal that belongs to me.
- Dogs gnaw bones.
- I admit no animals into my study, unless they will beg when told to do so.
- All the animals in the yard are mine.
- I admit every animal that I trust into my study.
- The only animals that are really willing to beg when told to do so are dogs.

How are yard-animals and bone-gnawing logically related?

ANALOGY

Follow the logic of the first pair to find the closest corresponding option to complete the second pair.

NOMINATE is to CANDIDATE as CREATE is to:

a. Bey
b. Burgrave
c. Mayor
d. Cardinal

ANTONYM

Which of the six options is closest to an opposite meaning of the word below?

CONJECTURAL

cocksure
fixed
singular
abounding
peremptory
intent

PUZZLE **108**

CIPHER

The block of text below represents a quotation that has been encrypted using a simple cipher. Can you decrypt it? You shouldn't need to use a computer to solve this puzzle, although there are some web sites that would help.

> WLMG HZB BLF WLMG SZEV VMLFTS GRNV BLF SZEV VCZXGOB GSV HZNV MFNYVI LU SLFIH KVI WZB GSZG DVIV TREVM GL SVOVM PVOO-VI KZHGVFI NRX SZVOZMTVOL NLGSVI GVIVHZ OVLMZIWL WZ ERMXR GSLNZH QVUUVIHLM ZMW ZOYVIG VRMH GVRM S QZXPHLM YILDM

CUT-UP

The lines below form a quotation attributed to a famous individual. Full-stops and commas have been removed, and the lines jumbled up. Can you piece the original quotation back together?

COMPLETE ABOLITION AS ITS

FRIEND AND FOE HAS RENDERED

I HAVE LONG ADVOCATED ITS

SETTLING INTERNATIONAL DISPUTES

IT USELESS AS A METHOD OF

NOTHING TO ME IS MORE REVOLTING

I KNOW WAR AS FEW OTHER MEN

NOW LIVING KNOW IT AND

VERY DESTRUCTIVENESS ON BOTH

Ernest Hemingway

PUZZLE **110**

DITLOID

A well-known phrase or title has been reduced to numbers and abbreviations in the clue below. Can you decipher the answer?

$$40 = W$$

PUZZLE **111**

DOUBLET

Change one letter at a time to form a new valid English word until you have transformed the first word into the second word.

There are 6 interim stages.

Bread

Toast

FOUR FROM FOUR

Within the four words below, four smaller words are hiding. What is the theme that unites them?

Dishabille

Glossolalia

Unsurprised

Counsellors

GAP-WORD

Which word will add to the two words below, to the end of the former, and the beginning of the latter to make two new words?

Task — ? — Fully

PUZZLE **114**

GRIDRUNNER

Starting from one spot in the grid below, move from letter to letter horizontally, vertically or diagonally to touch every letter once and spell out the name of a well-known person.

M	A	I	W	O
H	I	L	S	N
N	E	L	R	I
R	Y	H	A	R

PUZZLE **115**

HOLE

Fit a letter into the gap to complete four five-letter words.

AN___RA

TO___ES

IC___US

ME___AL

INTERMINGLING

Three loosely related words or phrases have been mixed together below. They are still in the right order, but each is scrambled with the other two. What are they?

```
F J O R T A H H N N F I K O M L
T Z I N G D E R E L A S J F A
N A L E O R D F K O E R O E N
S N E S O E V D Y E L N T
```

JUMBLE

The letters below form a well-known quotation. Each word has been anagrammed, and then the punctuation and spaces have been removed. The words are still in their correct places, however. Can you work out what the original quotation was? To help, we've given you the quotation's author.

```
V I G E E M A L E R E V N O G L H N E U G O D
A N A M U C F L R U O N C H H W I O T A C L E
P T I N A D L A H S L V O E M H E T L W D R O
```

Archimedes

PUZZLE **118**

KIN

In this puzzle, you have a group of five related words. One word in the other group belongs with them. Which one is it?

PASTORALE	Venus
TOLTEC	Mars
LAUDON	Jupiter
HAFFNER	Saturn
PATHÉTIQUE	Neptune

PUZZLE **119**

LETTERS

Rearrange the letters to form a single eight-letter word.

B
E
L
Y
S
C
I
C

LOGIC

Consider the statements below, and assuming that they are all perfectly true, answer the question that follows.

- Animals that do not kick are always unexcitable.
- Donkeys have no horns.
- A buffalo can always toss one over a gate.
- No animals that kick are easy to swallow.
- No hornless animal can toss one over a gate.
- All animals are excitable, except buffaloes.

How are donkeys and edibility related?

ODD ONE OUT

Which of the following words does not fit with the other four – and why? The answer lies in-the words' meanings.

Contraction

Homophone

Assonance

Alliteration

Onomatopoeia

PUZZLE **122**

PREFIXES

Which word can be added to the front of the following words to make five new whole words?

Tic

Arid

Final

Trailers

Fluid

PUZZLE **123**

SCRAMBLE

Remove one letter from each group in turn, going round three times, to spell out three different ten-letter words without re-using any letters.

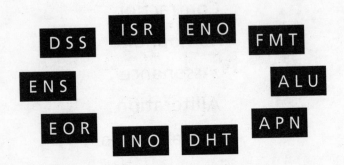

SELECTOR

Starting anywhere, pick one letter from each group in turn, clockwise, to find a ten-letter word loosely associated with night.

SEQUENCES

Work out the rationale behind the following sequence of letters and find the next one in the list.

M

M L J A

R F C

?

PUZZLE **126**

SYZYGY

Transform the first word into the second by moving from word to word. Each new word must share a continuous group of at least three letters – the 'link' – with the word before it.

Abbreviations, names, foreign words, compound words and slang are all forbidden. Consecutive links may overlap by a maximum of one letter, and similarly you may only use one letter of common suffixes and prefixes – such as '-ing', '-ers' or 'un-' – in a link. No link words may be longer than 11 letters.

There are 2 in-between syzygies.

Converse

Cheerfully

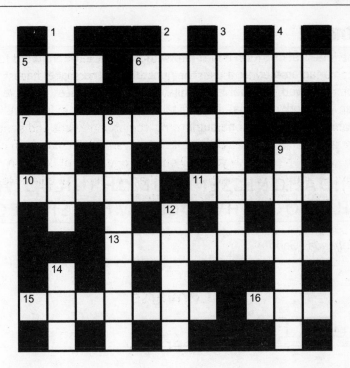

Across

5. Sounds like she's on top of the scales (3)
6. Alan re-hears the confusion (7)
7. Red, twisted Guianans (8)
10. National crimes (5)
11. Orthodox philosophy is about conjunction (5)
13. Such girlish feet (8)
15. Shoot down the street (5–2)
16. Thamesly eyot (3)

Down

1. Vassal promises great things (7)
2. Thai creators from that time (5)
3. A bit bigger than bandoliers? (8)
4. Who says the Welsh are fat? (3)
8. Baking powder, for instance? (8)
9. Single-sex herbiage (7)
12. Spain's most ardent supporter (5)
14. Sanskrit illuminant (3)

PUZZLE 128

JUMBLE

The letters below form a well-known quotation. Each word has been anagrammed, and then the punctuation and spaces have been removed. The words are still in their correct places, however. Can you work out what the original quotation was? To help, we've given you the quotation's author.

```
FIIDAHONESSENOFUMOHRUILUOWD
NLOGOGAEHVAOCDTIMMETSIDUECI
```

Mohandas Gandhi

PUZZLE 129

DITLOID

A well-known phrase or title has been reduced to numbers and abbreviations in the clue below. Can you decipher the answer?

1 = MW to M (W to M a M)

PREFIXES

Which word can be added to the front of the following words to make five new whole words?

Grave
Fall
Wards
Less
Mark

SEQUENCES

Work out the rationale behind the following sequence of letters and find the next one in the list.

PUZZLE **132**

ANALOGY

Follow the logic of the first pair to find the closest corresponding option to complete the second pair.

SKELF is to SPLINTER as TRENDLE is to:

a. Pail
b. Ring
c. Table
d. Helmet

PUZZLE **133**

ANTONYM

Which of the six options is closest to an opposite meaning of the word below?

NOMINATED

unknown
hazy
esoteric
intricate
impenetrable
fuliginous

CIPHER

The block of text below represents a quotation that has been encrypted using a simple cipher. Can you decrypt it? You shouldn't need to use a computer to solve this puzzle, although there are some web sites that would help.

LVOSRG   QFJUDQ   VLGRRG   HXVLHX   YCHXUK

BNKIXT   QDDQQF   EWHXLV   QFJUWZ   RGEWHX

DQWZKI   RGQDHX   ZOKIHX   UKHXYC   HXUKLV

IYLVQF   GRQDBN   VLHXOS   IYQDDQ   BNDQDQ

QFJUHX   OSRGXT

PUZZLE **135**

CUT-UP

The lines below form a quotation attributed to a famous individual.
Full-stops and commas have been removed, and the lines jumbled
up. Can you piece the original quotation back together?

AT THE HUGE WAVES OF THE SEA

CIRCULAR MOTIONS OF THE

AT THE LONG COURSES OF

MEN GO ABROAD TO WONDER AT

THEMSELVES WITHOUT WONDERING

STARS AND THEY PASS BY

COMPASS OF THE OCEAN AT THE

THE HEIGHTS OF MOUNTAINS

THE RIVERS AT THE VAST

Saint Augustine

DITLOID

A well-known phrase or title has been reduced to numbers and abbreviations in the clue below. Can you decipher the answer?

1 = B in the H is WT in the B

DOUBLET

Change one letter at a time to form a new valid English word until you have transformed the first word into the second word.

There are 6 interim stages.

Black

White

PUZZLE **138**

FOUR FROM FOUR

Within the four words below, four smaller words are hiding. What is the theme that unites them?

Interlocutor

Defilement

Propensities

Semiconductors

PUZZLE **139**

GAP-WORD

Which word will add to the two words below, to the end of the former and the beginning of the latter, to make two new words?

Document — ? — Gate

GRIDRUNNER

Starting from one spot in the grid below, move from letter to letter horizontally, vertically or diagonally to touch every letter once and spell out the name of a well-known person.

D	M	R	S
O	O	A	H
G	U	L	A
R	H	T	L

HOLE

Fit a letter into the gap to complete four five-letter words.

JA__ES

MA__ER

PE__OE

CO__ES

PUZZLE **142**

INTERMINGLING

Three loosely related words or phrases have been mixed together below. They are still in the right order, but each is scrambled with the other two. What are they?

V O M E B L U N T C A S E N E N O B
O L R O U O L O G R G N I E S R Y T

PUZZLE **143**

JUMBLE

The letters below form a well-known quotation. Each word has been anagrammed, and then the punctuation and spaces have been removed. The words are still in their correct places, however. Can you work out what the original quotation was? To help, we've given you the quotation's author.

N R E E V O R Y W R U T A B O H Y T R E S A
N G L O A S H E T H A N R Y I C M
S D O E A H T W I T S D S U S E P O P O T D O

Robert A. Heinlein

KIN

In this puzzle, you have a group of five related words. One word in the other group belongs with them. Which one is it?

BUS	pinch
WHALES	wicket
BARN	foe
ELEPHANT	machine
JUPITER	gravel

LETTERS

Rearrange the letters to form a single eight-letter word.

R

H

I

T

T

I

L

S

PUZZLE **146**

LOGIC

Consider the statements below, and assuming that they are all perfectly true, answer the question that follows.

- No one who is going to a party ever fails to brush his or her hair.
- No one looks fascinating if he or she is untidy.
- Alcoholics have no self-command.
- Everyone who has brushed hair looks fascinating.
- No one wears white kid gloves unless he or she is going to a party.
- A person is always untidy, if he or she has no self-command.

How are alcoholics and white kid gloves logically related?

PUZZLE **147**

ODD ONE OUT

Which of the following words does not fit with the other four – and why? The answer lies in the words' meanings.

Hierarchy
Judgement
Pronounciation
Twelfth
Accommodate

PREFIXES

Which word can be added to the front of the following words to make five new whole words?

Away
Out
Man
Over
About

SCRAMBLE

Remove one letter from each group in turn, going round three times, to spell out three different ten-letter words without re-using any letters.

PUZZLE **150**

SELECTOR

Starting anywhere, pick one letter from each group in turn, clockwise, to find a ten-letter word loosely associated with crafts.

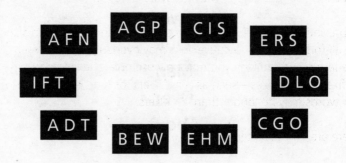

PUZZLE **151**

SEQUENCES

Work out the rationale behind the following sequence of letters and find the next one in the list.

B D G

K P

?

SYZYGY

Transform the first word into the second by moving from word to word. Each new word must share a continuous group of at least three letters – the 'link' – with the word before it.

Abbreviations, names, foreign words, compound words and slang are all forbidden. Consecutive links may overlap by a maximum of one letter, and similarly you may only use one letter of common suffixes and prefixes – such as '-ing', '-ers' or 'un-' – in a link. No link words may be longer than 11 letters.

There are 3 in-between syzygies.

Lead

Bullets

Across

- **5.** Droop (3)
- **6.** Setting (7)
- **7.** Used (4-4)
- **10.** Acclaim (5)
- **11.** Computer communication (1–4)
- **13.** Faineance (8)
- **15.** Slum (5,2)
- **16.** Start (3)

Down

- **1.** Beat (7)
- **2.** Rebound (5)
- **3.** Kin (8)
- **4.** Hollow (3)
- **8.** Remnants (8)
- **9.** Gooey (7)
- **12.** Formerly popular (5)
- **14.** Flirt (3)

ODD ONE OUT

Which of the following words does not fit with the other four – and why? The answer lies in the words' meanings.

Subfusc

Zeugma

Boskage

Nugatory

Heggle

INTERMINGLING

Three loosely related words or phrases have been mixed together below. They are still in the right order, but each is scrambled with the other two. What are they?

```
C R B E L A N A U T D T Y L I E R N I A
W N T A I I T G O I R N A N S M G
```

PUZZLE **156**

SCRAMBLE

Remove one letter from each group in turn, going round three times, to spell out three different ten-letter words without re-using any letters.

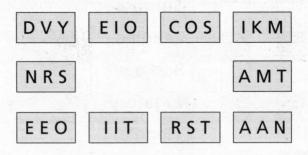

D V Y	E I O	C O S	I K M
N R S			A M T
E E O	I I T	R S T	A A N

PUZZLE **157**

LOGIC

Consider the statements below, and assuming that they are all perfectly true, answer the question that follows.

- Animals are always mortally offended if I fail to notice them.
- The only animals that belong to me are in that field.
- No animal can guess a conundrum, unless it has been properly trained in a Boarding School.
- None of the animals in that field are badgers.
- When an animal is mortally offended, it always rushes about wildly and howls.
- I never notice any animal, unless it belongs to me.
- No animal that has been properly trained in a Boarding School ever rushes about wildly and howls.

How are badgers and conundrums logically related?

ANALOGY

Follow the logic of the first pair to find the closest corresponding option to complete the second pair.

HAZARD is to GAIN as PINCH is to:

          a. Wake
          b. Snap
          c. Lose
          d. Steal

ANTONYM

Which of the six options is closest to an opposite meaning of the word below?

REPINE

cavil
leave
allot
thwart
straighten
praise

PUZZLE **160**

CIPHER

The block of text below represents a quotation that has been encrypted using a simple cipher. Can you decrypt it? You shouldn't need to use a computer to solve this puzzle, although there are some web sites that would help.

EWZZO	VHXQF	EWZBN	RBNHX	YDQUK
OVLIY	NUKRG	EQDQF	DRGZO	EBNRG
SXATZ	IOLVO	RSOSE	EWHXQ	SDRGU
TKHXG	ORLVV	LLDQS	IHSHR	VGLVQ
EFWZH	LXGRE	OWBNW	NZKIH	GXWZK
BILVQ	UFJUV	TLBNR	NGXTG	ORLVG
ORQFW	NZGRR	EGWZK	WIDQQ	OFEWB
UNWZK	LIHXR	DGQFH	BXVLB	ENRGX
OTGRL	LVGRV	DLRGW	AZKIU	BKRGZ
RORGI	AYIYW	HZKIH	AXEWR	MGZOO
LSLVQ	IFHXV	NLVLD	CQLVO	OSDQZ
LODQB	NNIYU			

CUT-UP

The lines below form a quotation attributed to a famous individual. Full-stops and commas have been removed, and the lines jumbled up. Can you piece the original quote back together?

ARISTOCRACY OR MONARCHY

DEMOCRACY WHILE IT LASTS

THAT DID NOT COMMIT SUICIDE

LASTS LONG IT SOON WASTES

IS MORE BLOODY THAN EITHER

REMEMBER DEMOCRACY NEVER

EXHAUSTS AND MURDERS ITSELF

THERE IS NEVER A DEMOCRACY

John Adams

PUZZLE **162**

DITLOID

A well-known phrase or title has been reduced to numbers and abbreviations in the clue below. Can you decipher the answer?

50 = W to LYL

PUZZLE **163**

DOUBLET

Change one letter at a time to form a new valid English word until you have transformed the first word into the second word.

There are 6 interim stages.

O n e

T w o

FOUR FROM FOUR

Within the four words below, four smaller words are hiding. What is the theme that unites them?

Incapacitated

Patriarchate

Peculiarities

Prototyping

GAP-WORD

Which word will add to the two words below, to the end of the former and the beginning of the latter, to make two new words?

War — ? — Ships

PUZZLE **166**

GRIDRUNNER

Starting from one spot in the grid below, move from letter to letter horizontally, vertically or diagonally to touch every letter once and spell out the name of a well-known person.

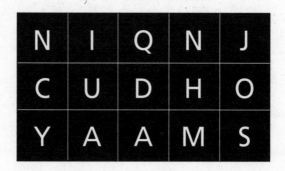

PUZZLE **167**

HOLE

Fit a letter into the gap to complete four five-letter words.

KE__FS

JU__OR

FE__NY

TO__US

INTERMINGLING

Three loosely related words or phrases have been mixed together below. They are still in the right order, but each is scrambled with the other two. What are they?

```
A R C O M A N M S I Y U S S U G N E M R M E
E N T P N L A T S R U S S T C H A O D O E R E P
```

JUMBLE

The letters below form a well-known quotation. Each word has been anagrammed, and then the punctuation and spaces have been removed. The words are still in their correct places, however.

Can you work out what the original quotation was?
To help, we've given you the quotation's author.

```
A D H T E O E S D O N T C N O C E N R U S
A U C S B E E S A G N O L A S E W E S I T X D
E H T A S I O T N E R H E D N A H E W N T I E
D S O O M C E E W O N O L R G N E E S X T I
```

Epicurus

PUZZLE **170**

KIN

In this puzzle, you have a group of five related words. One word in the other group belongs with them. Which one is it?

CLIMATE	teen
TROOPER	village
SQUIDGY	art
WATER	nanny
CABLE	strong

PUZZLE **171**

LETTERS

Rearrange the letters to form a single eight-letter word.

N E G I S T Z I

LOGIC

Consider the statements below, and assuming that they are all perfectly true, answer the question that follows.

- No husband, who is always giving his wife new dresses, can be a cross-grained man.
- A methodical husband always comes home for his tea.
- No one who hangs up his hat on the gas-jet can be a man that is kept in proper order by his wife.
- A good husband is always giving his wife new dresses.
- No husband can fail to be cross-grained, if his wife does not keep him in proper order.
- An unmethodical husband always hangs up his hat on the gas-jet.

How are good husbands and their tea related?

ODD ONE OUT

Which of the following words does not fit with the other four – and why? The answer lies in the words' meanings.

Calcanei

Hallux

Nares

Pollices

Glosso

PUZZLE **174**

PREFIXES

Which word can be added to the front of the following words to make five new whole words?

Plasm

Cortex

Phobia

Natal

Colonial

PUZZLE **175**

SCRAMBLE

Remove one letter from each group in turn, going round three times, to spell out three different ten-letter words without re-using any letters.

BFD	EES
IIR	NRW
ANO	EIO
ABI	ERS
DLT	DSS

SELECTOR

Starting anywhere, pick one letter from each group in turn,
clockwise, to find a ten-letter word loosely associated with sport.

SEQUENCES

Work out the rationale behind the following sequence of letters
and find the next one in the list.

A D B C
D D E
D ?

PUZZLE **178**

SYZYGY

Transform the first word into the second by moving from word to word. Each new word must share a continuous group of at least three letters – the 'link' – with the word before it.

Abbreviations, names, foreign words, compound words and slang are all forbidden. Consecutive links may overlap by a maximum of one letter, and similarly you may only use one letter of common suffixes and prefixes – such as '-ing', '-ers' or 'un-' – in a link. No link words may be longer than 11 letters.

There are 3 in-between syzygies.

Dog

Cat

Across

2. Slide (4)
4. Beam (7)
5. Crescendo (6)
7. Hide (4)
8. Sways (4)
9. Flow against (4)
11. Thrash (4)
14. Vocalist (6)
15. Rummage (7)
16. Row (4)

Down

1. Universe (6)
2. Halt (4)
3. Curve-billed wader (4)
4. Bohemian dance (5)
6. Horizontal line (1-4)
9. Carriage with two-part roof (6)
10. Low-cut front (1,4)
12. Catch (4)
13. Spread (4)

PUZZLE **180**

JUMBLE

The letters below form a well-known quotation. Each word has been anagrammed, and then the punctuation and spaces have been removed. The words are still in their correct places, however. Can you work out what the original quotation was? To help, we've given you the quotation's author.

**OYUTACNETGAPCUFOETAGIBGNOUE
HROAOBOKGNLONGHEUOOTUSTIEM**

C. S. Lewis

PUZZLE **181**

DITLOID

A well-known phrase or title has been reduced to numbers and abbreviations in the clue below. Can you decipher the answer?

$$22 = C$$

PREFIXES

Which word can be added to the front of the following words to make five new whole words?

Card

Mate

Me

Way

Mose

SEQUENCES

Work out the rationale behind the following sequence of letters and find the next one in the list.

C

O P A

L E F L W

O E G

?

PUZZLE **184**

ANALOGY

Follow the logic of the first pair to find the closest corresponding option to complete the second pair.

YELLOW is to ATTENTIVE as BLUE is to:

a. Enthusiastic
b. Romantic
c. Calm
d. Fertile

PUZZLE **185**

ANTONYM

Which of the six options is closest to an opposite meaning of the word below?

SEMBLANCE

source
formless
difference
ersatz
ghast
allusion

CIPHER

The block of text below represents a quotation that has been encrypted using a simple cipher.

Can you decrypt it? You shouldn't need to use a computer to solve this puzzle, although there are some web sites that would help.

25552	79751	91969	64956	59763	95933	92594
69594	91177	69525	49279	28592	89571	97639	49452
94692	81592	79285	96551	97639	49491	69289
65966	69285	92653	95519	11939	15179	69649
28591	16598	19269	93123	89285	92914	59595
41995	97639	91193	19567	36959	49514	94192
92519	50000					

CUT-UP

The lines below form a quotation attributed to a famous individual.
Full-stops and commas have been removed, and the lines jumbled
up. Can you piece the original quote back together?

AS I WAS SURE I KNEW EXACTLY

WHAT WAS HAPPENING AT THE

ON A MONITOR IN MY BEDROOM

I'M THE TYPE WHO'D BE HAPPY

I'M THE TYPE WHO'D LIKE TO

PARTY THAT I'M INVITED TO

NOT GOING ANYWHERE AS LONG

PLACES I WASN'T GOING TO

SIT HOME AND WATCH EVERY

Andy Warhol

DITLOID

A well-known phrase or title has been reduced to numbers and abbreviations in the clue below. Can you decipher the answer?

$$10 = RP$$

DOUBLET

Change one letter at a time to form a new valid English word until you have transformed the first word into the second word.

There are 6 interim stages.

Grass

Green

FOUR FROM FOUR

Within the four words below, four smaller words are hiding. What is the theme that unites them?

Reappeared

Stealthiest

Shibboleth

Scornfully

PUZZLE **191**

GAP-WORD

Which word will add to the two words below, to the end of the former and the beginning of the latter, to make two new words?

Keel — ? — Load

GRIDRUNNER

Starting from one spot in the grid below, move from letter to letter horizontally, vertically or diagonally to touch every letter once and spell out the name of a well-known person.

HOLE

Fit a letter into the gap to complete four five-letter words.

TU___ES

HE ___AD

BO___ER

SA ___ON

PUZZLE 194

JUMBLE

The letters below form a well-known quotation. Each word has been anagrammed, and then the punctuation and spaces have been removed. The words are still in their correct places, however. Can you work out what the original quotation was? To help, we've given you the quotation's author.

I K I L E G N L O W K A S L L Y L E I A S
C E P N H E W E H Y T R A E T E -
KAY   B P E P E L O H O W N O A Y N E M

Fred Allen

PUZZLE 195

INTERMINGLING

Three loosely related words or phrases have been mixed together below. They are still in the right order, but each is scrambled with the other two. What are they?

A H A M U P L N H T S R I B O A L I O I U
G M H T S V C E C R H A I A C B F L T E

KIN

In this puzzle, you have a group of five related words. One word in the other group belongs with them. Which one is it?

MANOS   Battletoads

INCHON   Supertrain

BIRDEMIC   Ryantown

EEGAH   Eldorado

GIGLI   North

LETTERS

Rearrange the letters to form a single eight-letter word.

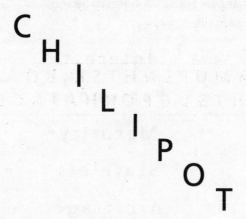

C H I L I P O T

PUZZLE **198**

LOGIC

Consider the statements below, and assuming that they are
all perfectly true, answer the question that follows.

- Everything that is not absolutely ugly may be kept in a drawing-
  room.
- Nothing that is encrusted with salt is ever quite dry.
- Nothing should be kept in a drawing-room, unless it is
  free from damp.
- Bathing-machines are always kept near the sea.
- Nothing that is made of mother-of-pearl can be absolutely ugly.
- Whatever is kept near the sea gets encrusted with salt.

How are bathing-machines and mother-of-pearl logically related?

PUZZLE **199**

ODD ONE OUT

Which of the following words does not fit with the other four – and
why? The answer lies in the words' meanings.

Interest

Parsimony

Maturity

Stateless

Arbitrage

PREFIXES

Which word can be added to the front of the following words to make five new whole words?

Aged

Man

Thread

Horse

Sack

SCRAMBLE

Remove one letter from each group in turn, going round three times, to spell out three different ten-letter words without re-using any letters.

IMR EIT ANY
BRV ANY
EII ELN
LTT EOQ
AIS BGU
LIT

PUZZLE **202**

SELECTOR

Starting anywhere, pick one letter from each group in turn, clockwise, to find a ten-letter word loosely associated with art.

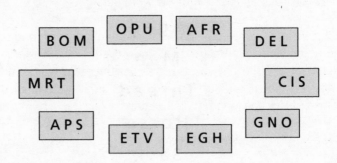

PUZZLE **203**

SEQUENCES

Work out the rationale behind the following sequence of letters and find the next one in the list.

AR | TA | GE | CA | LE | VI | ?

SYZYGY

Transform the first word into the second by moving from word to word. Each new word must share a continuous group of at least three letters – the 'link' – with the word before it.

Abbreviations, names, foreign words, compound words and slang are all forbidden. Consecutive links may overlap by a maximum of one letter, and similarly you may only use one letter of common suffixes and prefixes – such as '-ing', '-ers' or 'un-' – in a link. No link words may be longer than 11 letters.

There are 3 in-between syzygies.

Spread

Banquet

Across

6. Stop (5)
7. Aggressive (5)
8. Unit of electrical resistance (3)
10. Balconied tower (7)
11. Axe (7)
13. Crossly (7)
15. Drunk (3)
16. Small paddle-boat (5)
17. Fairies (5)

Down

1. Numberwork (11)
2. Loner (6)
3. Pie (4)
4. Rubble (8)
5. Order (11)
9. Burnt sienna (8)
12. Tomboy (6)
14. Chilly (4)

ODD ONE OUT

Which of the following words does not fit with the other four – and why? The answer lies in the words' meanings.

Adulate

Hypocorism

Dedolence

Digamy

Uxorious

INTERMINGLING

Three loosely related words or phrases have been mixed together below. They are still in the right order, but each is scrambled with the other two. What are they?

```
P S Y E P E D R T I R M O I C E L N A F I S
T A T I E R Y D C F W R O L O O W C K O D
```

PUZZLE **208**

LOGIC

Consider the statements below, and assuming that they are all perfectly true, answer the question that follows.

- I never put a cheque, received by me, on that file, unless I am anxious about it.
- All the cheques received by me, that are not marked with a cross, are payable to bearer.
- None of them are ever brought back to me, unless they have been dishonoured at the Bank.
- All of them, that are marked with a cross, are for amounts of over £100.
- All of them, that are not on that file, are marked "not negotiable".
- No cheque of yours, received by me, has ever been dishonoured.
- I am never anxious about a cheque, received by me, unless it should happen to be brought back to me.
- None of the cheques received by me, that are marked "not negotiable", are for amounts of over £100.

How is a cheque of yours and the cheque's bearer logically related?

SCRAMBLE

Remove one letter from each group in turn, going round three times, to spell out three different ten-letter words without re-using any letters.

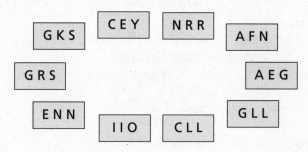

ANALOGY

Follow the logic of the first pair to find the closest corresponding option to complete the second pair.

VOLUBLE is to CHATTY as BOBCAT is to:

a. Cougar

b. Ocelot

c. Serval

d. Lynx

PUZZLE 211

ANTONYM

Which of the six options is closest to an opposite meaning of the word below?

EIDOLON

creature
deception
whole
analogy
corpse
vision

PUZZLE 212

CIPHER

The block of text below represents a quotation that has been encrypted using a simple cipher. Can you decrypt it? You shouldn't need to use a computer to solve this puzzle, although there are some web sites that would help.

```
VMOVE  VIUBL  FWTLZ  GSORM  TGUSL  FTTSR
GXDZM  MVAEV  IYMVP  MLNDM  YFSGG  LBPLF
IHOVO  UZTHP  BLWFI  HVIOU  SLLDB  LFLDL
FOIWZ  XGADV  IVMZO  OGSSV  DLHIO  WOALL
PRKMT  ZGEBL  FZSMW  ZXPGZ  XXELI  WRAMT
OBRGS  LNEZH
```

CUT-UP

The lines below form a quotation attributed to a famous individual. Full-stops and commas have been removed, and the lines jumbled up. Can you piece the original quotation back together?

LANGUAGE IS INSINCERITY

A CUTTLEFISH SQUIRTING OUT INK

WORDS AND EXHAUSTED IDIOMS LIKE

DECLARED AIMS ONE TURNS AS

ONE'S REAL AND ONE'S

THE GREAT ENEMY OF CLEAR

IT WERE INSTINCTIVELY TO LONG

WHEN THERE IS A GAP BETWEEN

George Orwell

PUZZLE **214**

DITLOID

A well-known phrase or title has been reduced to numbers and abbreviations in the clue below. Can you decipher the answer?

$$24 = BB \text{ in a } P$$

PUZZLE **215**

DOUBLET

Change one letter at a time to form a new valid English word until you have transformed the first word into the second word.

There are 6 interim stages.

Elm

Oak

FOUR FROM FOUR

Within the four words below, four smaller words are hiding. What is the theme that unites them?

Acupuncture

Antipathies

Ranitidine

Researchers

GAP-WORD

Which word will add to the two words below, to the end of the former and the beginning of the latter, to make two new words?

Mode — ? — Able

Across

6. Clueless (9)
7. Hole punch (3)
8. Fuss (3)
9. Cheek (3)
11. Battered (3-4)
13. Sawbone (3)
14. Container (3)
16. Possesses (3)
17. Mall (9)

Down

1. Twitchy (8)
2. Nothing (4)
3. Ladies' fingers (4)
4. Asymmetrically ornamented (6)
5. Complete (4,2)
10. Nice (8)
11. Formula (6)
12. Honeyed nut paste (6)
15. Indian bread (4)
16. Pay attention (4)

GRIDRUNNER

Starting from one spot in the grid below, move from letter to letter horizontally, vertically or diagonally to touch every letter once and spell out the name of a well-known person.

Y	V	I	A
L	E	S	R
E	L	O	N
S	E	R	P

HOLE

Fit a letter into the gap to complete four five-letter words.

H I __ A B

B I __ O U

R A __ A S

D O __ O S

PUZZLE **221**

INTERMINGLING

Three loosely related words or phrases have been mixed together below. They are still in the right order, but each is scrambled with the other two. What are they?

```
Q U N S L O R I T P H E A P R K I N E
N R G R Y E A D E S O P E A L N M K
```

PUZZLE **221**

JUMBLE

The letters below form a well-known quotation. Each word has been anagrammed, and then the punctuation and spaces have been removed. The words are still in their correct places, however. Can you work out what the original quotation was? To help, we've given you the quotation's author.

```
E O S T H H O S E W I E F L I S N O G L T L
L I S S V R I E T R O F N A G I N A D O F R
L A L R L S O A M T L L A I T S G N H K A T
E O C N E S D E A L P C O T N M E O Y
```

Sophocles

KIN

In this puzzle, you have a group of five related words. One word in the other group belongs with them. Which one is it?

KYODU	adanaxis
CAMOGIE	buzkashi
TRUGO	krank
OINA	tong
PATBALL	nexuiz

LETTERS

Rearrange the letters to form a single eight-letter word.

L
A
D
E
N
R
A
S

PUZZLE **225**

LOGIC

Consider the statements below, and assuming that they are all perfectly true, answer the question that follows.

- I call no day "unlucky", when Robinson is pleasant to me.
- Wednesdays are always cloudy.
- When people take umbrellas, the day never turns out dry.
- The only days when Robinson is unpleasant to me are Wednesdays.
- Everybody takes their umbrella with them when it is raining.
- My "lucky" days always turn out dry.

How are cloudy and rainy days logically related?

PUZZLE **226**

ODD ONE OUT

Which of the following words does not fit with the other four – and why? The answer lies in the words' meanings.

Whitewash

Rabbit Ears

Monkey

Bisque

Cellar

PREFIXES

Which word can be added to the front of the following words to make five new whole words?

Way

Tone

Beak

Back

Times

SCRAMBLE

Remove one letter from each group in turn, going round three times, to spell out three different ten-letter words without re-using any letters.

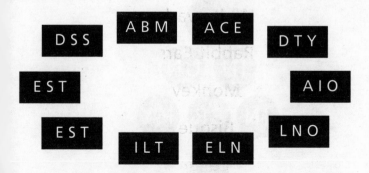

SELECTOR

Starting anywhere, pick one letter from each group in turn, clockwise, to find a ten-letter word loosely associated with fortune.

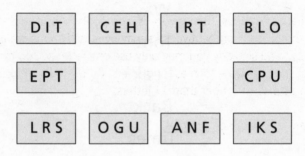

| D I T | C E H | I R T | B L O |

| E P T | | | C P U |

| L R S | O G U | A N F | I K S |

PUZZLE **230**

SEQUENCES

Work out the rationale behind the following sequence of letters and find the next one in the list.

SYZYGY

Transform the first word into the second by moving from word to word. Each new word must share a continuous group of at least three letters – the 'link' – with the word before it.

Abbreviations, names, foreign words, compound words and slang are all forbidden. Consecutive links may overlap by a maximum of one letter, and similarly you may only use one letter of common suffixes and prefixes – such as '-ing', '-ers' or 'un-' – in a link. No link words may be longer than 11 letters.

There are 3 in-between syzygies.

Demand

Cormorant

PUZZLE **232**

Across

5. Foes (10)
7. Told advantageously (4)
8. Gave (6)
9. Meat (5)
10. Type (5)
13. Clannish (6)
15. Mint (4)
16. Applied science (10)

Down

1. Chunks (6)
2. Close (5)
3. Pantera leo (4)
4. Inherent (10)
6. Being sought after (10)
11. Vellicate (6)
12. Unseeing (5)
14. Returned (4)

JUMBLE

The letters below form a well-known quotation. Each word has been anagrammed, and then the punctuation and spaces have been removed. The words are still in their correct places, however. Can you work out what the original quotation was? To help, we've given you the quotation's author.

```
I E N U R V E T O T Y S A O R A W A N C
B E O N L G E C R R A D I O N S A A N
I G T H T E I L W L F O H T E E P E L O P
```

Edmund Burke

DITLOID

A well-known phrase or title has been reduced to numbers and abbreviations in the clue below. Can you decipher the answer?

15 = M on a DMC

PUZZLE **235**

PREFIXES

Which word can be added to the front of the following words to make five new whole words?

Back

Face

Rage

Flank

Span

PUZZLE **236**

SEQUENCES

Work out the rationale behind the following sequence of letters and find the next one in the list.

C.	A	D	A	E	I	B	?

ANALOGY

Follow the logic of the first pair to find the closest corresponding option to complete the second pair.

HEAD is to CABBAGE as HEART is to:

a. Garlic
b. Onion
c. Mushroom
d. Celery

ANTONYM

Which of the six options is closest to an opposite meaning of the word below?

ABUTMENT

rupture
chunk
moiety
gap
variance
stretch

CIPHER

The block of text below represents a quotation that has been encrypted using a simple cipher. Can you decrypt it? You shouldn't need to use a computer to solve this puzzle, although there are some web sites that would help.

WEEEY	UOTIG	HUHTA	NVREN	WBTOO	REFSY
USLHW	OWUDC	WRALH	WRDOK	NAYUN	ATCOD
NLTOA	JFESN	HNVRO	DAHNT	OGICN	EEBKO
NUTYU	SLAKO	REFOY	UOLAT	EELTE	OLLOI
GTOAD	CACRI	GYHMS	EFROX		

CUT-UP

The lines below form a quotation attributed to a famous individual. Full-stops and commas have been removed, and the lines jumbled up. Can you piece the original quotation back together?

WHISPER SO THE MYSTIC

BREATHE FORTH THEIR LOVE

WERE CREEP INTO GOD

FOR EACH OTHER TO LET

JUST AS IN EARTHLY LIFE

WHEN THEY ARE ABLE TO

LONGS FOR THE MOMENT WHEN

THEIR SOULS BLEND IN A SOFT

LOVERS LONG FOR THE MOMENT

IN PRAYER HE CAN AS IT

Soren Kierkegaard

PUZZLE **241**

DITLOID

A well-known phrase or title has been reduced to numbers and abbreviations in the clue below. Can you decipher the answer?

1 = FO the CN

PUZZLE **242**

DOUBLET

Change one letter at a time to form a new valid English word until you have transformed the first word into the second word.

There are 8 interim stages.

Blue

Pink

FOUR FROM FOUR

Within the four words below, four smaller words are hiding. What is the theme that unites them?

Intermixed

Disowning

Subtleties

Consortiums

GAP-WORD

Which word will add to the two words below, to the end of the former and the beginning of the latter, to make two new words?

Stop — ? — Ants

PUZZLE **244**

GRIDRUNNER

Starting from one spot in the grid below, move from letter to letter
horizontally, vertically or diagonally to touch every letter once and
spell out the name of a well-known person.

PUZZLE **245**

HOLE

Fit a letter into the gap to complete four five-letter words.

NI __ IL

CO __ OE

AR __ AT

UN __ IP

INTERMINGLING

Three loosely related words or phrases have been mixed together below. They are still in the right order, but each is scrambled with the other two. What are they

```
A B V A M P U A R H D N I T E V I L
S H E T O A R L I T M E A R E R N
```

JUMBLE

The letters below form a well-known quotation. Each word has been anagrammed, and then the punctuation and spaces have been removed. The words are still in their correct places, however. Can you work out what the original quotation was? To help, we've given you the quotation's author.

```
S A O N L G A S O U Y E A T H E T R H
E L L W I E B E O P L P E O T H E T A
```

George Harrison

PUZZLE **249**

KIN

In this puzzle, you have a group of five related words. One word in the other group belongs with them. Which one is it?

TRUG	bushel
PERCH	drum
HOPPUS	modius
SLUG	talent
KENNING	weevil

PUZZLE **250**

LETTERS

Rearrange the letters to form a single eight-letter word.

F i t g o o s e

LOGIC

Consider the statements below, and assuming that they are all perfectly true, answer the question that follows.

- No shark ever doubts that it is well fitted out.
- A fish that cannot dance a minuet is contemptible.
- No fish is quite certain that it is well fitted out, unless it has three rows of teeth.
- All fishes, except sharks, are kind to children.
- No heavy fish can dance a minuet.
- A fish with three rows of teeth is not contemptible.

How are heavy fish and children logically related?

ODD ONE OUT

Which of the following words does not fit with the other four – and why? The answer lies in the words' meanings.

Arete

File

Fianchetto

Hypermodern

Zugzwang

PUZZLE **253**

PREFIXES

Which word can be added to the front of the following words to make five new whole words?

Boosh
Red
Sal
Tan
Weed

PUZZLE **254**

SCRAMBLE

Remove one letter from each group in turn, going round three times, to spell out three different ten-letter words without re-using any letters.

SELECTOR

Starting anywhere, pick one letter from each group in turn, clockwise, to find a ten-letter word loosely associated with cruelty.

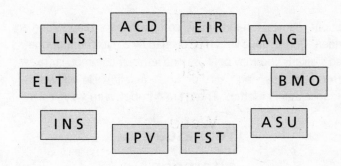

SEQUENCES

Work out the rationale behind the following sequence of letters and find the next one in the list.

PUZZLE **257**

SYZYGY

Transform the first word into the second by moving from word to word. Each new word must share a continuous group of at least three letters – the 'link' – with the word before it.

Abbreviations, names, foreign words, compound words and slang are all forbidden. Consecutive links may overlap by a maximum of one letter, and similarly you may only use one letter of common suffixes and prefixes – such as '-ing', '-ers' or 'un-' – in a link. No link words may be longer than 11 letters. There are 4 in-between syzygies.

Wednesday

Afternoon

PUZZLE **258**

INTERMINGLING

Three loosely related words or phrases have been mixed together below. They are still in the right order, but each is scrambled with the other two. What are they?

```
P C O L D N A O V D E T O X E P N C
O I L Y A H C S E O L G D R O I D O N N
```

Across

2. Version (7)
6. Smarten (5–2)
7. Fire dust (3)
8. Spin (5)
10. Weakness (5)
12. Playful water-mammal (5)
15. Teat (5)
17. Duplicator (3)
18. Escape (7)
19. Typo (7)

Down

1. Nativtity (5)
3. Official philosopher (5)
4. Subject (5)
5. Seventh Jewish month (5)
9. Regret (3)
11. Box (3)
13. Shadow (5)
14. Unreliable (5)
15. Radical (5)
16. Play out (5)a

ODD ONE OUT

Which of the following words does not fit with the other four – and why? The answer lies in the words' meanings.

Cumbia
Merengue
Hustle
Glissade
Beguine

PUZZLE 261

SCRAMBLE

Remove one letter from each group in turn, going round three times, to spell out three different ten-letter words without re-using any letters.

C O P	A H U	S T Y	C L S
D S Y			A O R
E R T	E E P	L P T	C O U

LOGIC

Consider the statements below, and assuming that they are all perfectly true, answer the question that follows.

- All the dated letters in this room are written on blue paper.
- None of them are in black ink, except those that are written in the third person.
- I have not filed any of them that I can read.
- None of them, that are written on one sheet, are undated.
- There is a precise overlap between crossed letters and black ink.
- All of them, written by Brown, begin with "Dear Sir".
- All of them, written on blue paper, are filed.
- None of them, written on more than one sheet, are crossed.
- None of them, that begin with "Dear Sir", are written in the third person.

How are Brown's letters and legibility logically related?

SOLUTIONS

Puzzle 1

C.

The dog is a member of the order of Carnivora.

Puzzle 2

The antonym of desolation, the deprivation of comfort and joy, is

'joy'.

Puzzle 3

The cipher is a very basic one to get you warmed up. It works by just removing spaces and breaking the resulting text into blocks of five letters. The last block is rounded up to five characters with junk. The quotation is:

All truly wise thoughts have been thought already thousands of times; but to make them truly ours, we must think them over again honestly, till they take root in our personal experience.

Johann Wolfgang von Goethe

Puzzle 4

The quotation is:

Books constitute capital. A library book lasts as long as a house, for hundreds of years. It is not, then, an article of mere consumption but fairly of capital, and often in the case of professional men, setting out in life, it is their only capital.

Thomas Jefferson

Puzzle 5

The phrase is "Seven Wonders of the Ancient World".

Puzzle 6

One solution is

HEAD – heal – teal – tell – tall – TAIL

Puzzle 7

The theme is types of insect, and the words are:

Ant

Bee

Tick

Moth

Puzzle 8

The gap-word is

piece

forming altarpiece and piecemeal.

SOLUTIONS

Puzzle 9
Arnold Schwarzenegger

Puzzle 10
L – calyx, balms, talus, helot

Puzzle 11
The Arctic Circle
International Date Line
Southern Hemisphere

Puzzle 12
"No matter how long he lives, no man ever becomes as wise as the average woman of forty-eight."

H. L. Mencken

Puzzle 13

Choose

Because it indicates the bestowal of favour.

Puzzle 14

The solution is

cryogens.

Puzzle 15

Rainbows are not worth writing odes to.

Puzzle 16

The odd one out is

appeal

The other four words all indicate placing blame.

SOLUTIONS

Puzzle 17
The prefix is

bio.

Puzzle 18
One answer is lutestring, chocolates and underscore.

Puzzle 19
Demolition

Puzzle 20
The next letter is

M

Each time, the letters move on by three.

Puzzle 21

One answer is

WALRUS – (rus) – peruse – (per) – harper – (arp) – CARPENTER.

Puzzle 22

Puzzle 23

"I've got a long list of books I wish I'd never written – and I've kept them all out of print for the past twenty years."

Dean Koontz

Puzzle 24

The phrase is "Seven Samurai" from the film by Akira Kurosawa.

SOLUTIONS

Puzzle 25

The prefix is

ear.

Puzzle 26

The next letter is

C

The sequence is made up of the letters of the standard abbreviations for the elements in increasing atomic weight: Hydrogen, HElium, LIthium, BEryllium, Boron and Carbon.

Puzzle 27

b. Cadmium.

It is the next element after Silver in the periodic table.

Puzzle 28

The antonym of enthetic, coming from an external source, is

internal.

Puzzle 29

The cipher works by simple substitution, moving each letter of the alphabet one space forward, so that A becomes B, B becomes C, and so on. Word breaks are left alone. The quotation is:

Anyone who stops learning is old, whether at twenty or eighty. Anyone who keeps learning stays young. The greatest thing in life is to keep your mind young.

Henry Ford

Puzzle 30

The quotation is:

For having lived long, I have experienced many instances of being obliged, by better information or fuller consideration, to change opinions, even on important subjects, which I once thought right but found to be otherwise.

Benjamin Franklin

Puzzle 31

The phrase is "Three Men in a Boat", from the book by Jerome K. Jerome.

Puzzle 32

One solution is

APE – apt – opt – oat – mat – MAN.

SOLUTIONS

Puzzle 33

The theme is types of animal, and the words are:

Cat

Dog

Pig

Rat

Puzzle 34

The gap-word is

sit

forming babysit and sitreps.

Puzzle 35

Diana Princess of Wales.

Puzzle 36

G – caged, eager, sagos, gigue.

Puzzle 37

Aeolian harp
tubular bells
upright piano

Puzzle 38

"As long as you're going to be thinking anyway, think big."

Donald Trump

Puzzle 39

Suzerainty

Because it is a type of controlled territory.

Puzzle 40

The solution is

paginate.

SOLUTIONS

Puzzle 41

The Sorites are difficult.

Puzzle 42

The odd one out is

murmalize

It is not a real word, although to 'marmalize' means to thrash. To fletcherize is to chew slowly and thoroughly; to absquatulate is to flee; to subtilize is to make more subtle or discerning; and to yaff is to yelp.

Puzzle 43

The prefix is

ring.

Puzzle 44

One answer is hematology, quesadilla and tourmaline.

Puzzle 45

Amanuensis.

Puzzle 46

The next letter is

S

The sequence is made up of the first letters of the even numbers in ascending order: Two, Four, Six, Eight, Ten, Twelve, Fourteen and Sixteen.

Puzzle 47

One answer is

INDULGE – (ndu) – unduly – (uly) – incredulity – (ncr) – IDIOSYNCRASY.

Puzzle 48

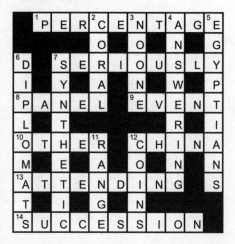

SOLUTIONS

Puzzle 49

Did you notice that the answer didn't lie with the meanings? The odd one out is 'tarts', which has a very low Scrabble score. The other four all have very high Scrabble scores.

Puzzle 50

pruning shears

measuring tape

monkey wrench

Puzzle 51

One answer is bromeliads observance and greenstone.

Puzzle 52

No driver lives on barley-sugar.

Puzzle 53

b. Johnson

Kennedy was succeeded by Johnson.

SOLUTIONS

Puzzle 54

The antonym of predicate, to declare openly, is

suppress.

Puzzle 55

The cipher works by simply reversing the entire block of text, so it starts with the last letter and reads back to the first. The quotation is:

If a man is called to be a street sweeper, he should sweep streets even as Michelangelo painted or Beethoven composed music or Shakespeare wrote poetry. He should sweep streets so well that all the hosts of heaven and earth will pause and say, "Here lived a great street sweeper who did his job well."

Martin Luther King, Jr.

Puzzle 56

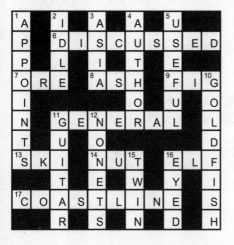

SOLUTIONS

Puzzle 57

The quotation is:

Security is mostly a superstition. It does not exist in nature, nor do the children of men as a whole experience it. Avoiding danger is no safer in the long run than outright exposure. Life is either a daring adventure, or nothing.

Helen Keller

Puzzle 58

The phrase is

Twelve Labours of Hercules.

Puzzle 59

One solution is

SLEEP – bleep – bleed – breed – bread – dread – DREAM.

Puzzle 60

The theme is body parts, and the words are

Arm

Ear

Lip

Leg

Puzzle 61

The gap-word is

head

forming redhead and headspring.

Puzzle 62

George Washington

Puzzle 63

P – moped, kapok, repot, aspic

Puzzle 64

micro-apartment
hunting lodge
boarding house

SOLUTIONS

Puzzle 65

"Many a trip continues long after movement in time and space have ceased."

John Steinbeck

Puzzle 66

Sargon, because he was known as 'the Great'.

Puzzle 67

The solution is

stabbing.

Puzzle 68

All my dreams come true.

SOLUTIONS

Puzzle 69

The odd one out is

carrel

a type of cubicle. The others are all forms of punctuation.

Puzzle 70

The prefix is

gall.

Puzzle 71

One answer is

lifeguards, pellucidly and hoodwinked.

Puzzle 72

Lexicality

SOLUTIONS

Puzzle 73

The next letter is

J

The sequence is made up of the first letters of the months in reverse order: December, November, October, September, August, July and June.

Puzzle 74

One answer is

COOK – (coo) – scooping – (pin) – pinned – (nne) – DINNER.

Puzzle 75

Puzzle 76

"Three things cannot be long hidden: the sun, the moon, and the truth."

Buddha

Puzzle 77

The phrase is

Four Horsemen of the Apocalypse.

Puzzle 78

The prefix is

mad.

Puzzle 79

The next letter is

F

The letters are a simple alphabetic sequence, subtracting one place after every three letters.

Puzzle 80

c. Crop

Irrigation results in a crop.

SOLUTIONS

Puzzle 81

The antonym of noose, to snare, is 'liberate'.

Puzzle 82

The cipher works by rotating each letter 13 places forward in the alphabet, known in computer circles as "ROT-13", so A becomes N, B becomes O, and so on. The quotation is:

History shows us that the people who end up changing the world -- the great political, social, scientific, technological, artistic, even sports revolutionaries -- are always nuts, until they are right, and then they are geniuses.

John Eliot

Puzzle 83

The quotation is:

The TV business is uglier than most things. It is normally perceived as some kind of cruel and shallow money trench through the heart of the journalism industry, a long plastic hallway where thieves and pimps run free and good men die like dogs, for no good reason.

Hunter S. Thompson

Puzzle 84

The phrase is "Two Gentlemen of Verona", from the play by William Shakespeare.

Puzzle 85

One solution is

FLOUR – floor – flood – blood – brood – broad – BREAD.

Puzzle 86

The theme is crime, and the words are:

Rob

Con

Gun

Cell

Puzzle 87

The gap-word is

berry

forming hackberry and berrylike.

Puzzle 88

Martin Luther King Jr

SOLUTIONS

Puzzle 89

B – sabot, debar, embow, rebus

Puzzle 90

triceratops
velociraptor
heterodontosaurus

Puzzle 91

"As is a tale, so is life: not how long it is, but how good it is, is what matters."

Lucius Annaeus Seneca

Puzzle 92

Jakob

because his name became associated with a disease or syndrome.

Puzzle 93

The solution is

Dadaists.

Puzzle 94

All the English pictures here are painted in oils.

Puzzle 95

The odd one out is 'the same page', which indicates agreement.
The others are all used to indicate problems.

Puzzle 96

The prefix is

ultra

SOLUTIONS

Puzzle 97

One answer is wirehaired, adulteries and handcuffed.

Puzzle 98

Shogunates

Puzzle 99

The next letter is E. The sequence is made up of the second letters of the integers in ascending order: oNe, tWo, tHree, fOur, fIve, sIx and sEven.

Puzzle 100

One answer is

KNIFE – (nif) – manifest – (man) – workman – (ork) – FORK.

Puzzle 101

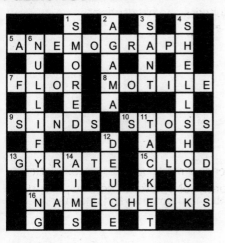

Puzzle 102

The odd one out is 'antelope'. The other four animals – the kodiak is a bear, and the gaur is an ox – are all very heavy and ponderous, whilst the antelope is notably light and springy.

Puzzle 103

espadrilles
platform shoes
Wellington boots

Puzzle 104

One answer is ecumenists, motherhood and reabsorbed.

SOLUTIONS

Puzzle 105

All the animals in the yard gnaw bones.

Puzzle 106

d

Cardinals are 'created'.

Puzzle 107

The antonym of conjectural, being theoretical and uncertain, is

fixed.

Puzzle 108

The cipher works by switching letters of the alphabet with the letters that would be in their position if the alphabet was reversed, so in other words A becomes Z, B becomes Y, and so on. The quotation is:

Don't say you don't have enough time. You have exactly the same number of hours per day that were given to Helen Keller, Pasteur, Michaelangelo, Mother Teresa, Leonardo da Vinci, Thomas Jefferson, and Albert Einstein.

H. Jackson Brown

Puzzle 109

The quotation is:

I know war as few other men now living know it, and nothing to me is more revolting. I have long advocated its complete abolition, as its very destructiveness on both friend and foe has rendered it useless as a method of settling international disputes.

Ernest Hemingway

SOLUTIONS

Puzzle 110

The phrase is

Forty Winks.

Puzzle 111

One solution is

BREAD – break – bleak – bleat – blest – blast – boast – TOAST.

Puzzle 112

The theme is business, and the words are:

Bill

Loss

Rise

Sell

Puzzle 113

The gap-word is

master

forming taskmaster and masterfully.

Puzzle 114

William Henry Harrison

Puzzle 115

T – antra, totes, ictus, metal

Puzzle 116

Franklin Delano Roosevelt

John Fitzgerald Kennedy

Thomas Jefferson

Puzzle 117

"Give me a lever long enough and a fulcrum on which to place it, and I shall move the world."

Archimedes

SOLUTIONS

Puzzle 118

Jupiter

because it is the name of a symphony.

Puzzle 119

The solution is

bicycles.

Puzzle 120

Donkeys are not easy to swallow.

Puzzle 121

The odd one out is

contraction

The others are all related to the sound of words.

Puzzle 122

The prefix is

semi.

Puzzle 123

One answer is rotundness, inflations and semaphored.

Puzzle 124

Hypnogogic

Puzzle 125

The next term

SC

The sequence is made up of the first letters of the books of the New Testament: Matthew, Mark, Luke, John, Acts, Romans, First Corinthians and Second Corinthians.

SOLUTIONS

Puzzle 126

One answer is

CONVERSE – (ers) – persevering – (per) – perfumery – (rfu) – CHEERFULLY.

Puzzle 127

Puzzle 128

"If I had no sense of humour, I would long ago have committed suicide."

Mohandas Gandhi

Puzzle 129

The phrase is "One Man Went to Mow (Went to Mow a Meadow)".

Puzzle 130

The prefix is

land.

Puzzle 131

The next term is

CH

The sequence is made up of the first two letters of the English counties in alphabetical sequence: AVon, BEdfordshire, BErkshire, BUckinghamshire, CAmbridgeshire and CHeshire.

Puzzle 132

b. Ring

A trendle is a type of ring.

Puzzle 133

The antonym of nominated, being famed, is 'unknown'.

SOLUTIONS

Puzzle 134

The cipher works on the basis of simple substitution, but each single letter of the original is replaced with the same 2-letter pair. The first letter of each pair is three places along from the original. So A becomes DQ, B becomes EW, and so on. The quotation is:

I long, as does every human being, to be at home wherever I find myself.

Maya Angelou

Puzzle 135

The quote is:

Men go abroad to wonder at the heights of mountains, at the huge waves of the sea, at the long courses of the rivers, at the vast compass of the ocean, at the circular motions of the stars, and they pass by themselves without wondering.

Saint Augustine

Puzzle 136

The phrase is "A Bird in the Hand is Worth Two in the Bush."

Puzzle 137

One solution is

BLACK – blank – blink – clink – chink – chine – whine – WHITE.

Puzzle 138

The theme is computing, and the words are:

Cut

File

Open

Icon

Puzzle 139

The gap-word is

able

forming documentable and ablegate.

Puzzle 140

Thurgood Marshall

Puzzle 141

K – jakes, maker, pekoe, cokes

SOLUTIONS

Puzzle 142

meteorologist

volcanology

bunsen burner

Puzzle 143

"Never worry about theory as long as the machinery does what it's supposed to do."

Robert A. Heinlein

Puzzle 144

Foe

because it is an unconventional unit of measurement.

Puzzle 145

The solution is

triliths.

Puzzle 146

No alcoholic ever wears white kid gloves.

Puzzle 147

The odd one out is 'pronounciation', which is misspelt, and should be 'pronunciation'. The others are spelt correctly, although they are frequently misspelt.

Puzzle 148

The prefix is

walk.

Puzzle 149

One answer is incubating, bandleader and cinerarium.

SOLUTIONS

Puzzle 150

Crocheting

Puzzle 151

The next letter is

V

The sequence starts at B, and each time, the gap between letters increases by 1.

Puzzle 152

One answer is

LEAD – (ead) – plead – (ple) – sample – (sam) – jetsam – (ets) – BULLETS.

Puzzle 153

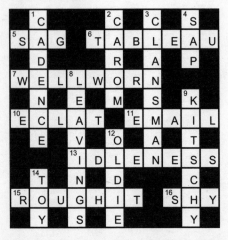

SOLUTIONS

Puzzle 154

The odd one out is 'heggle', which is not a real word. Subfusc means dingy, a boskage is a thicket of shrubs, nugatory means worthless or trifling, and a zeugma occurs when a word is used to govern two or more words, often in different senses. For instance, from the humorous song 'Have Some Madeira, M'dear' by Michael Flanders: "She lowered her standards by raising her glass, her courage, her eyes and his hopes."

Puzzle 155

crenulations

lady-in-waiting

battering ram

Puzzle 156

One answer is

dockmaster, visitation and yeomanries.

Puzzle 157

No badger can guess a conundrum.

SOLUTIONS

Puzzle 158

a. Wake

Waking from a dream can require a pinch, allegedly.

Puzzle 159

The antonym of repine, to moan or complain, is 'praise'.

Puzzle 160

The cipher works by misdirection. Only the first letter of each five-letter block means anything. These first letters spell out the quote in the correct order. The quotation is:

Every one desires to live long, but no one would be old.

Abraham Lincoln

CU7

Puzzle 161

The quotation is:

Democracy, while it lasts, is more bloody than either aristocracy or monarchy. Remember, democracy never lasts long. It soon wastes, exhausts, and murders itself. There is never a democracy that did not commit suicide.

John Adams

Puzzle 162

The phrase is "Fifty Ways to Leave Your Lover", from the song by Paul Simon.

Puzzle 163

One solution is

ONE – ope – opt – out – tut – tot – too – TWO.

Puzzle 164

The theme is clothing, and the words are:

Cap

Hat

Tie

Pin

Puzzle 165

The gap-word is

head

forming warhead and headships.

SOLUTIONS

Puzzle 166

John Quincy Adams

Puzzle 167

R – kerfs, juror, ferny, torus

Puzzle 168

army surplus store
amusement arcade
consignment shop

Puzzle 169

"Death does not concern us, because as long as we exist, death is not here. And when it does come, we no longer exist."

Epicurus

Puzzle 170

Nanny, because with the suffix -gate, it was the popular term for a scandal.

Puzzle 171

The solution is

zingiest.

Puzzle 172

A good husband always comes home for his tea.

Puzzle 173

The odd one out is 'glosso', which is used as a prefix in compound words to chiefly indicate speech and words. The other four are medical terms for specific pieces of anatomy. Calcanei are heels, the hallux is the big toe, the nares are the nostrils and the pollices are the thumbs. The corresponding term for tongue is 'glossa'.

SOLUTIONS

Puzzle 174

The prefix is

neo

Puzzle 175

One answer is diableries, broadsword and finiteness.

Puzzle 176

Tobogganer

Puzzle 177

The next letter is

F

It is a simple alphabetical sequence with an extra 'D' added every two letters after the first such addition.

SOLUTIONS

Puzzle 178

One answer is

DOG – (dog) – endogen – (gen) – gentry – (ntr) – intricate – (cat) – CAT.

Puzzle 179

Puzzle 180

"You can't get a cup of tea big enough or a book long enough to suit me."

C. S. Lewis

Puzzle 181

The phrase is

Catch 22

from the book by Joseph Heller.

SOLUTIONS

Puzzle 182

The prefix is

race.

Puzzle 183

The next term is WO. The sequence is made up of the first two letters of the traditional gifts for wedding anniversaries in ascending chronological order: COtton, PAper, LEather, FLowers & Fruit, WOod, EGg and WOol.

Puzzle 184

c. Calm

Blue is said to make you calm.

Puzzle 185

The antonym of semblance, a likeness of form, is 'difference'.

SOLUTIONS

Puzzle 186

The cipher works by replacing the letters of the alphabet with the numbers 1-9 in order. Once the alphabet reaches J, it starts from 1 again. So A, J and T are all represented by '1'. The last '9' in the sequence is used to replace spaces in the original. The quotation is:

Twenty years from now you will be more disappointed by the things you didn't do than by the ones you did. So throw off the bowlines, sail away from the safe harbor. Catch the trade winds in your sails. Explore. Dream.

Mark Twain

Puzzle 187

The quotation is:

I'm the type who'd be happy not going anywhere as long as I was sure I knew exactly what was happening at the places I wasn't going to. I'm the type who'd like to sit home and watch every party that I'm invited to on a monitor in my bedroom.

Andy Warhol

Puzzle 188

The phrase is

Ten Rillington Place

from the book by Ludovic Kennedy.

SOLUTIONS

Puzzle 189

One solution is

GRASS – crass – cress – tress – trees – treed – greed – GREEN.

Puzzle 190

The theme is colour, and the words are:

Red

Teal

Bole

Corn

Puzzle 191

The gap-word is

boat

forming keelboat and boatload.

Puzzle 192

Dwight Eisenhower

Puzzle 193

X – tuxes, hexad, boxer, Saxon

SOLUTIONS

Puzzle 194

"I like long walks, especially when they are taken by people who annoy me."

Fred Allen

Puzzle 195

amphibious vehicle
hansom cab
ultra-light craft

Puzzle 196

North

Because it was a movie that received a lot of negative attention and performed poorly.

Puzzle 197

The solution is

hoplitic.

SOLUTIONS

Puzzle 198

Bathing-machines are never made of mother-of-pearl.

Puzzle 199

The odd one out is 'parsimony', or miserliness; the other four are all terms used by the finance industry.

Puzzle 200

The prefix is

pack.

Puzzle 201

One answer is equilibria, negativity and lobstermen.

Puzzle 202

Lightproof

Puzzle 203

The next term is

LI

The sequence is made up of the first two letters of the signs of the zodiac in traditional order: ARies, TAurus, GEmini, CAncer, LEo, VIrgo and LIbra.

Puzzle 204

One answer is

SPREAD – (rea) – readiness – (ine) – shines – (shi) – vanquishing – (nqu) – BANQUET.

Puzzle 205

SOLUTIONS

Puzzle 206

The odd one out is 'dedolence', which indicates apathy; all the others are terms that imply a good relationship. To adulate is to show devotion, a hypocorism is a pet name or a piece of baby-talk, digamy is the practice of taking a second spouse (after a divorce or death), and to be uxorious is to be doting towards one's wife.

Puzzle 207

pyroclastic flow
sedimentary rock
petrified wood

Puzzle 208

All cheques of yours, received by me, are payable to bearer.

Puzzle 209

One answer is scragglier, gyrfalcons and kennelling.

Puzzle 210

a. Cougar.

A bobcat is a cougar.

Puzzle 211

The antonym of eidolon, an insubstantial phantom, is 'creature'.

Puzzle 212

The cipher is another misdirection. This time, the quotation is spelled by just the middle letters of each five-letter block. The quotation is:

Out, out, damn spot!

William Shakespeare

Puzzle 213

The quotation is:

The great enemy of clear language is insincerity. When there is a gap between one's real and one's declared aims, one turns, as it were, instinctively to long words and exhausted idioms, like a cuttlefish squirting out ink.

George Orwell

SOLUTIONS

Puzzle 214

The phrase is "Four and Twenty Blackbirds Baked in a Pie".

Puzzle 215

One solution is

ELM – ell – eel – bel – bet – bat – oat – OAK

Puzzle 216

The theme is restaurants, and the words are:

Cup

Tip

Dine

Sear

Puzzle 217

The gap-word is

rate

forming moderate and rateable.

Puzzle 218

Puzzle 219

Elvis Aron Presley

Puzzle 220

J – hijab, bijou, Rajas, dojos

Puzzle 221

northern red oak

quaking aspen

slippery elm

SOLUTIONS

Puzzle 222

"Those whose life is long still strive for gain, and for all mortals all things take second place to money."

Sophocles

Puzzle 223

Buzkashi

Because it is a sport.

Puzzle 224

The solution is

adrenals.

Puzzle 225

Rainy days are always cloudy.

Puzzle 226

The odd one out is 'monkey'. The others are all terms used in sport. A whitewash is a complete and utter defeat, Rabbit Ears indicates a sportsman who is easily riled by taunts and jibes, a bisque is an extra turn or free point, and the cellar is the lowest spot on a sporting ladder.

Puzzle 227

The prefix is

half.

Puzzle 228

One answer is actionless, medallists and bayoneted.

Puzzle 229

Auspicious

SOLUTIONS

Puzzle 230

The next term is NI. The sequence is made up of the first two letters of the nations of the world in decreasing order of population size: CHina, INdia, UNited States, INdonesia, BRazil, PAkistan and NIgeria.

Puzzle 231

One answer is

DEMAND – (ema) – gentleman – (ent) – tangent – (ang) – orange – (ora) – CORMORANT.

Puzzle 232

SOLUTIONS

Puzzle 233

"I venture to say no war can be long carried on against the will of the people."

Edmund Burke

Puzzle 234

The phrase is "Fifteen Men on a Dead Man's Chest".

Puzzle 235

The prefix is

out.

Puzzle 236

The next term is F. The sequence is obtained by substituting the letters A-I for the respective digits 1–9 into the value of Pi:

3.1415926.

Puzzle 237

d. Celery

You can buy celery hearts.

SOLUTIONS

Puzzle 238

The antonym of abutment, the meeting of two ends, is 'gap'.

Puzzle 239

The cipher works by transposition. The text is broken up into two segments, made up by alternating the letters of the original. So the sequence ABCDEFGHIJ would break up into ACEGI BDFHJ. The quotation is:

Whenever you do a thing, though it can never be known but to yourself, ask yourself how you would act, were all the world looking at you, and act accordingly.

Thomas Jefferson

Puzzle 240

The quotation is:

Just as in earthly life lovers long for the moment when they are able to breathe forth their love for each other, to let their souls blend in a soft whisper, so the mystic longs for the moment when in prayer he can, as it were, creep into God.

Soren Kierkegaard

Puzzle 241

The phrase is "One Flew Over the Cuckoo's Nest" from the book by Ken Kesey.

Puzzle 242

One solution is

BLUE – glue – glut – gout – pout – port – part – pant – pint – PINK.

Puzzle 243

The theme is gardening, and the words are:

Mix
Sow
Tie
Sort

Puzzle 244

The gap-word is

page

forming stoppage and pageants.

Puzzle 245

Coretta Scott King

SOLUTIONS

Puzzle 246

H – nihil, cohoe, Arhat, unhip

Puzzle 247

amphitheatre
barnstormer
vaudevillian

Puzzle 248

"As long as you hate, there will be people to hate."

George Harrison

Puzzle 249

Bushel, because it is an imperial unit of measurement.

Puzzle 250

The solution is

goofiest.

Puzzle 251

No heavy fish is unkind to children.

Puzzle 252

The odd one out is 'arete', which means good character – its close cousin arête is a sharp mountain ridge, incidentally. The other words are all used in chess. A file is a vertical line of squares on a board; fianchetto is the process of freeing up the bishop in an opening move by advancing an appropriate pawn; hypermodern refers to game history of the current times; and a zugzwang is a position where the player's next moves all have a negative outcome.

Puzzle 253

The prefix is

tar.

SOLUTIONS

Puzzle 254

One answer is minefields, frictional and acidophile.

Puzzle 255

Villainous

Puzzle 256

The next letter is

P

The sequence is made up of pairs of adjacent letters split by two-letter gaps, starting from D.

Puzzle 257

One answer is

WEDNESDAY – (edn) – blessedness – (sse) – finesse – (ine) – craftiness – (raf) – rafter – (fte) – AFTERNOON.

Puzzle 258

Platonic solid

dodecahedron

convex polygon

Puzzle 259

Puzzle 260

The odd one out is

glissade

a type of gliding step used in ballet. The other four are all specific dances.

SOLUTIONS

Puzzle 261

One answer is outcropped, cassoulets and phylactery.

Puzzle 262

I cannot read any of Brown's letters.